Cockroach's night out

by Clint Twist

Copyright © ticktock Entertainment Ltd 2006
First published in Great Britain in 2006 by ticktock Media Ltd.,
Unit 2, Orchard Business Centre, North Farm Road, Tunbridge Wells, Kent, TN2 3XF
We would like to thank: Indexing Specialists (UK) Ltd for their help with this project.
ISBN 1 86007 843 5 pbk
Printed in China
A CIP catalogue record for this book is available from the British Library.

Picture Credits
Alamy: 5b (Paul Heartfield), 17 (James Caldwell), 20-21 (Bruce Coleman Inc.). Ardea: 4 (Alan Weaving),
8b (Pat Morris). FLPA: 1, 15 side panel, 21 side panel, 23 side panel (Nigel Cattlin), 5t (Mark Moffett/Minden Pictures), 7 side
panel (Albert Mans/Foto Natura), 9, 13b, 19t (B. Borrell Casals). Getty Images: 11 side panel (Burke/Triolo Productions).
Nature Picture Library: 8 main (Nick Garbutt), 15 (Pete Oxford). The Natural History Museum, London: 23 middle.
OSF: 2-3, 22 (Colin Milkins), 12 (Phototake Inc), 13t. Premaphotos Wildlife: 14l, 14-15, 19 side panel, 26, 27b (Ken Preston-
Mafham). Science Photo Library: 11t (Barbera Strnadova), 16 (Volker Steger), 19b (Dr Morely Read), 21t (Jeff Lepore),
23t (Martin Dohrn), 27t (George Bernard).
Every effort has been made to trace the copyright holders, and we apologise in advance for any unintentional omissions.
We would be pleased to insert the appropriate acknowledgements in any subsequent edition of this publication.

CONTENTS

What are cockroaches?

Cockroaches are winged insects. They like warm, damp, dirty places. Cockroaches can run very quickly. They are very tough and do not squash easily.

How do they live?

Cockroaches either live alone or in small family groups consisting of a female and her young. They are normally only seen at night.

A mountain cockroach with nymphs 1-2 hours old.

What do they eat?

Cockroaches have very wide-ranging appetites – they will feed on just about any plant or animal material as long as it is already dead. Animals that live in this way are known as scavengers.

A Madagascan hissing
cockroach on the forest floor.

Where do they live?

Cockroaches like to live in warm,
damp conditions. Most cockroaches
live in tropical and sub-tropical
forests. Some cockroaches,
however, have invaded human
settlements and are now found
in cities throughout the world.

Understanding minibeasts

Insects belong to a
group of minibeasts
known as arthropods.
Adult arthropods have
jointed legs but do not have
an inner skeleton made of
bones. Instead, they have a
tough outer "skin" called an
exoskeleton that supports
and protects their bodies.
All insects have six legs
when they are adults, and
most also have at least one
pair of wings for flying,
although some have
two pairs.

Cockroaches have six legs
and are insects.

Cockroaches love to eat rotting fruit.

A cockroach up close

The average cockroach is about 2-4 cm long and is reddish-brown in colour. It has a tough outer covering that gives this minibeast a smooth, shiny appearance.

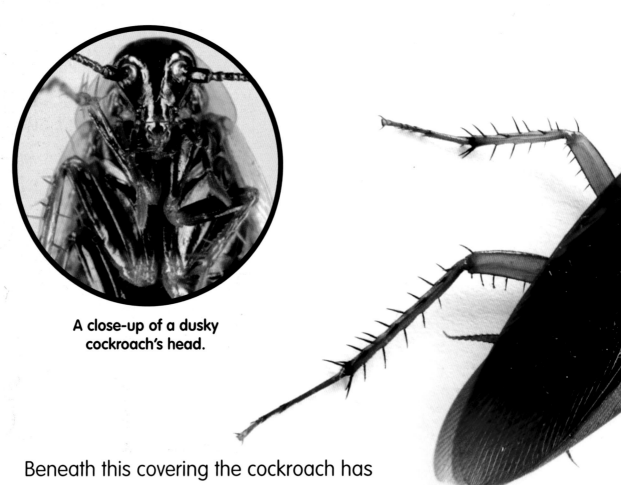

A close-up of a dusky cockroach's head.

Beneath this covering the cockroach has the same kind of body as all other adult insects. It is divided into three parts – head, thorax, and abdomen.

The head has antennae, eyes, a mouth and part of the brain. The rest of the brain is scattered along the underside of the body. Most insects have a mouth that points forwards or downwards, but a cockroach's mouth points backwards.

The head is often hidden from sight beneath a protective shield called a pronotum.

The thorax is the middle part of the body. The legs and wings are attached here.

The abdomen is the largest part of the cockroach's body. It contains the digestive system.

Six legs

Beetles and other insects are sometimes called hexapods because they all have six legs (hex means six in Latin). This definition is correct, but it is not the whole story. All insects are hexapods, but not all hexapods are insects. Some other minibeasts, such as springtails, have six legs but they are not true insects.

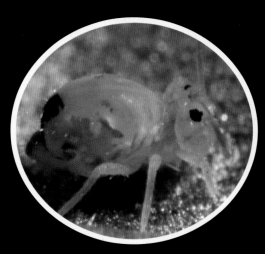

Springtails have six legs but they are not insects. Cockroaches also have six legs and they are insects.

Unfussy Eaters

Cockroaches are not carnivores (meat-eaters), and they are not herbivores (plant-eaters). These minibeasts are omnivores, which means that they will eat any kind of plant or animal food – but only if it is already dead.

This giant Madagascan hissing cockroach is eating rotting plants on the forest floor.

American cockroaches will eat animal droppings.

Cockroaches are not predators that hunt and kill other animals for food. Cockroaches are scavengers. They prefer their food to be not just dead, but rotting.

Rotting, or decomposition, is when microbes (which are known as decomposers) break down dead animals and plants.

An Oriental cockroach feeding on an insect.

Animals and plants gradually turn soft and mushy as they decompose – and cockroaches just love to eat this soft, mushy, partly decomposed stuff. Most cockroaches will also feed happily on animal droppings.

Cockroaches are part of nature's clean up crew. They help get rid of rotting animals, plants, and animal droppings

Log life

Some cockroaches, which are known as wood roaches, specialise in feeding on fallen trees. Wood, even rotten wood, is a very poor quality food. Wood roaches are able to live on this poor diet thanks to a particular microbe that lives in their digestive system. As a result, wood roaches do not have to go out in search of food – they can spend their whole lives safely inside a single rotten log.

A wood roach spends its whole life in a log, eating the rotting wood.

Getting Around

During the daytime, cockroaches hide from predators. Their flattened bodies help the insects squeeze into the smallest hiding places, where they wait for darkness.

At night, the cockroaches come out to feed. Although there are fewer predators around, the roaches still move very quickly. In fact, when it comes to walking and running, cockroaches are about the fastest things on six legs.

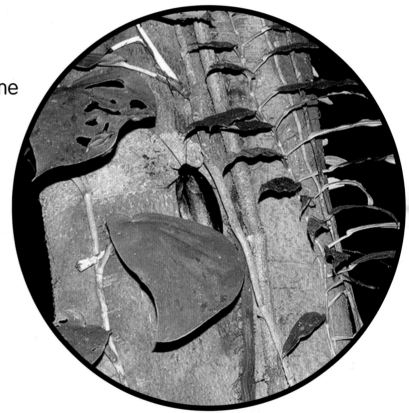

Cockroaches walk in the same way as other insects – they lift the middle leg on one side at the same time as the front and back legs on the opposite side. This means that there are always three legs touching the ground, which makes the insect very stable and unlikely to fall over.

When cockroaches run, they do not change the pattern of their steps.

In order to go from a walk to a run, insects just have to make their legs go faster. They do not have to change their pattern of steps the way horses change from a walk to a canter.

Horses use a different pattern of steps depending on how fast they want to go.

Insect sprinters

When cockroaches run, they really run! They lean back and lift the front of their bodies into the air so that they end up sprinting on just their back legs. At full speed, some cockroaches can cover up to 50 body lengths per second – about 10 times faster than a human runner.

Cockroaches are very fast sprinters, and run on their back legs.

Finding Food

Cockroaches have very poor eyesight, and some of them can do little more than tell the difference between light and dark. But they make up for this by having long antennae that have many sensitive receptors.

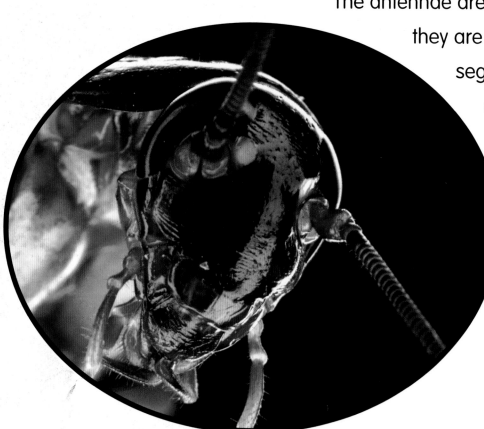

The antennae are very flexible because they are divided into about 100 segments. Each segment carries lots of sensitive receptors that the cockroach uses to find out about its surroundings.

The antennae on the head of this American cockroach are divided into about 100 segments.

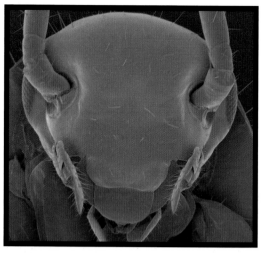

A cockroach's antennae act as ears and noses as well as 'feelers.' This is an American cockroach.

Some of the receptors are sensitive to vibration – not just the vibrations caused by movement, but also the vibrations of sound travelling through the air. Other receptors are sensitive to temperature, and there are separate receptors for hot and cold.

The most important receptors are those that allow cockroaches to sample smells. Different receptors can sense different smells, especially the distinctive smells made by decomposition.

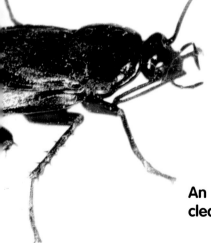

An Oriental cockroach cleaning its antennae.

Sensitive legs

In addition to their antennae, cockroaches can also detect vibrations through tiny bristles on their legs. Even while their antennae are busy finding food, their legs are alert to the slightest movements around them.

The hairs on a cockroach's leg can detect the slightest movement.

Bad Habits

Cockroaches are not nice to be around. For one thing, cockroaches make a bad smell. However bad the smells of rotting meat or plants, cockroaches can smell even worse.

Some cockroaches use their smell as a self-defence weapon. If threatened by a predator, they can squirt out a cloud of foul-smelling liquid. When the predator retreats from the bad smell, the cockroaches can easily escape.

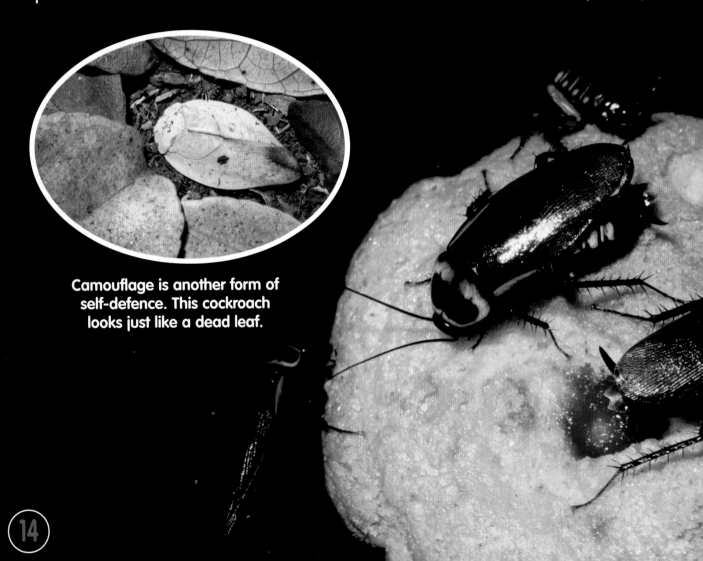

Camouflage is another form of self-defence. This cockroach looks just like a dead leaf.

This cockroach's self-defence system failed - it's being eaten by a scorpion!

Never mind the smell

What makes cockroaches really unpleasant neighbours, even to animals with no sense of smell, is the fact that they lack any form of toilet training. They leave a non-stop trail of droppings wherever they walk. Because their mouths point backwards, cockroaches have to walk all over their food in order to eat it. They even leave droppings on food they have not eaten.

Whatever the meaning to other roaches, the message to other animals is very clear – "Avoid this unpleasant insect."

The bad smell a cockroach makes might be a message to other cockroaches saying, "Here is plenty of food." Or it might have the opposite meaning, "Keep away, this food is mine."

These Australian cockroaches are feeding on a cake.

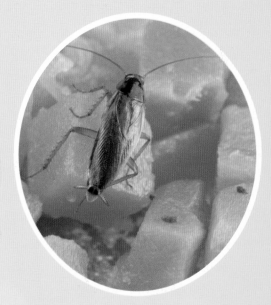

A German cockroach walking over food and leaving droppings.

infrequent Flyers

Both male and female cockroaches have wings, but the females of most cockroach species cannot fly. Only males have wings that can be used for flying, but they do not use them very often.

Most of the time, male and female cockroaches live completely separate lives. At mating time, the females release special smell substances that are known as pheromones. These substances mix with the air and get carried away with the wind.

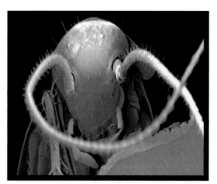

A German cockroach like this one, will use his antennae to detect a female.

Some of the smell receptors on the male cockroach's antennae can detect the faintest trace of these female pheromones.

Once the female pheromones have reached the male, he takes to the air and begins following the invisible pheromone trail back towards the waiting female.

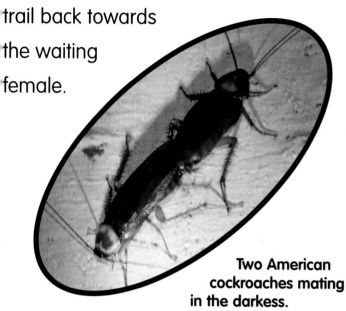

Two American cockroaches mating in the darkess.

If the male cannot find the female straight away, he lands and releases his own pheromones. These are not as strong as the female's, but they act in the same way and help the female find the male in the darkness.

Most cockroaches cannot fly, this male American cockroach only uses his wings to find a mate.

Females only

Not all minibeasts have to mate in order to produce young. Some insect species, such as the Surinam roach, are all female and they can produce fertile eggs without the need for any males. This process is known as parthenogenesis.

The Surinam roach does not need a male to reproduce.

Egg cases

There are over 4000 varieties of cockroaches. After mating, most female cockroaches lay their eggs inside a special egg case called an ootheca. Depending on the species of cockroach, there can be 6-50 eggs neatly arranged in an ootheca.

Some types of cockroaches carry the ootheca around with them for a few days, before leaving it in a suitably dark and damp place. Other kinds of cockroaches, however, continue to carry the ootheca for up to several weeks until their eggs hatch.

A smoky brown cockroach's ootheca.

All oothecae have an outer surface which is smooth and leathery, with a raised seam called a keel along one edge. Tiny openings at the base of the keel allow the eggs inside to breathe.

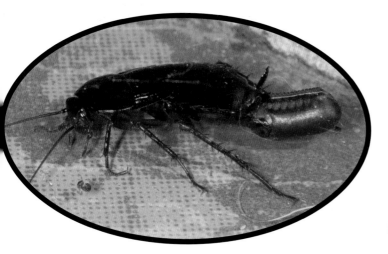

An Oriental cockroach with its ootheca.

Only a few types of cockroaches do not lay their eggs at all. Instead, the eggs develop inside the female's abdomen. The young cockroaches, called nymphs, are born live and not as eggs.

A female cockroach which has just given birth to her live young. This type of cockroach lives in Trinidad.

Insect development

Insects develop from eggs in two different ways. With many kinds of insect, including cockroaches and grasshoppers, the eggs hatch into nymphs that already have the adult body shape. However, with many other kinds of insect, such as bees and beetles, the eggs hatch into larvae that look very different from the adults. The larvae then go through a stage called pupation when they change into adults.

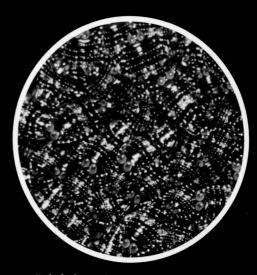

Brightly coloured cockroach nymphs in Kenya.

Nymph's Progress

Young cockroach nymphs look like miniature versions of the adults, but they are far from complete. It can take up to 10 months for nymphs to reach adulthood. During this time the youngsters will shed their "skin" a number of times.

This cockroach has just shed its exoskeleton (the white cockroach shape).

Insects have an exoskeleton that supports and protects their bodies. Exoskeletons are strong and tough, but they do not stretch. In order for the insect to grow in size, it must grow a new exoskeleton before shedding the outgrown one.

An Oriental cockroach nymph.

An eastern milk snake shedding its skin.

The process by which an animal sheds its outer covering is known as moulting. This term is not only used with insects and other arthropods, it is also used with some animals that have internal skeletons, such as snakes.

Newly hatched cockroach nymphs are pale and almost colourless, but they soon begin to turn darker. The youngsters will go through as many as 12 moults before they are fully adult. The stages between each moult are known as instars.

Staged growth

With each instar, the nymphs become more detailed and complete. For example, newly hatched nymphs have no wings at all, and their antennae have only about 25 segments compared with the 100 or so segments on adult antennae. Until the nymph reaches its final stage of growth, its wings and antennae will not be fully functional.

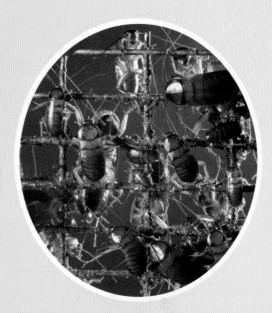

Adult and nymph American cockroaches.

Cockroaches & Humans

Cockroaches are most at home in warm, wet woodlands, but a long time ago they found out that human settlements are equally inviting.

Houses that are designed to be comfortable for people are also very comfortable for cockroaches. They provide everything the roaches need – heat, dampness, and large amounts of organic waste (unwanted bits of plants and animals).

Some cockroach species, about 20 in total, are so closely attached to human settlements that they have become serious pests. These cockroaches are now found in almost every town and city in the world.

American cockroaches are a serious pest to humans.

Among the worst pests are the German cockroach (which actually comes from Africa), the Oriental cockroach, and the American cockroach. These insects are often found living under floors and between walls, especially in bathrooms and kitchens.

German cockroach

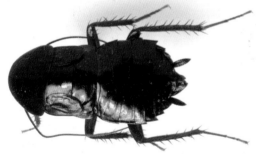

Oriental cockroach

American cockroach

Spoilage

Cockroaches are pests not only because of the food they eat, but also because of the food they spoil. Because of their bad habit of crawling all over the food and scattering droppings everywhere, cockroaches spoil about a thousand times more food than they actually consume.

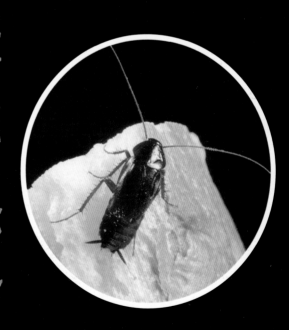

An Oriental cockroach crawling over (and spoiling) a piece of bread.

Unusual Behaviour

Some cockroaches do some fairly unusual things – well, unusual for cockroaches. Not only can the largest species grow to an amazing 7 cm, but the fastest cockroaches are entered into races by their human owners.

Hissing monster

The Madagascan giant cockroach is not only one of the biggest roaches at about 7 cm in length it is also the noisiest – so noisy in fact, that it uses sound as a defensive weapon. When this cockroach is disturbed, it repeatedly puffs its body up with air and then huffs out the air through tiny openings on its body surface. The air makes a loud hissing sound as it comes out. This is often enough to scare predators, giving the giant cockroach time to escape.

Parental care

Most young cockroaches do not get any parental care. But this is not the case with wood roaches. When these nymphs hatch, they do not have the microbes that allow them to feed on wood. At first, the nymphs have to stay close to their mother and feed on her droppings. These droppings contain the microbes which will allow the roaches to feed on wood. Only after several weeks do the nymphs have enough of the microbes to start feeding on wood.

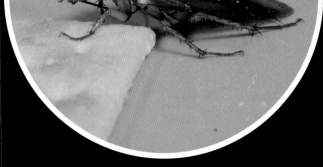

Fast runners

Many cockroaches can run fairly quickly, but none are faster than the American cockroach. This amazing insect can cover a distance of 150 cm in one second – about five times faster than a German cockroach, which can only cover about 30 cm in one second.

Cockroach sport

In some places cockroach racing is a well-organised sport. Races are run in daylight around a circular track. According to the rules, roaches that do not start running straight away may be prodded into action.

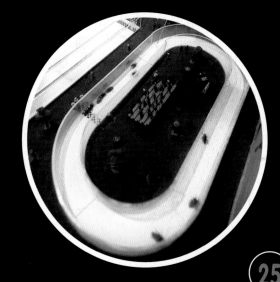

Sizes & Shapes

Although most cockroaches have the same basic body parts, there is a considerable variety of shape, size and colour.

Leaf cockroach

This West African cockroach hides from daytime predators by standing on the forest floor and keeping very still. It is perfectly camouflaged as a fallen yellow leaf, complete with one area that appears to be gradually turning brown.

Tropical giant cockroach

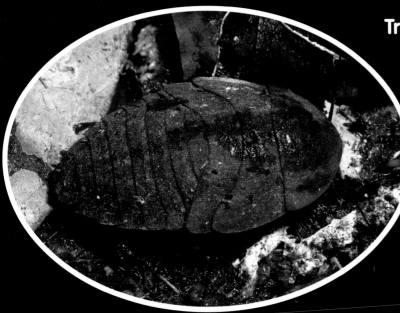

This cockroach from the tropical forests of Central America is one of the largest cockroaches in the world, and when fully grown can measure more than 7.5 cm in length.

Banana roach

The green banana roach does not invade houses, but is considered a pest because it feeds on crops.

Aptera fusca

The Cape Mountain cockroach lives in highland forest near the southern tip of Africa. Unlike most other cockroaches, the Cape Mountain cockroach does not lay its eggs in an ootheca. Instead the eggs remain inside the female's body until the nymphs hatch.

Find out More
Lifecycle

Most female cockroaches lay their eggs in a special case called an ootheca. The eggs hatch into nymph instars, which moult about 12 times before becoming fully grown adults.

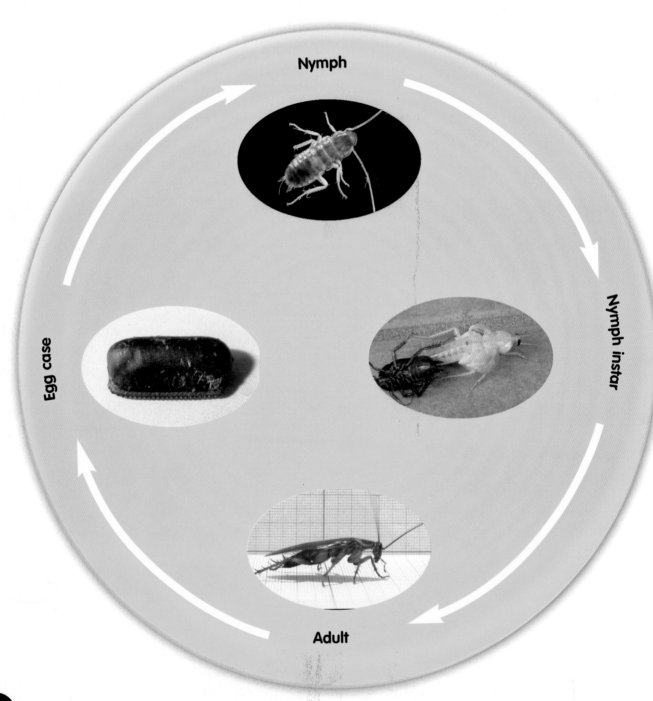

Nymph

Nymph instar

Adult

Egg case

Fabulous Facts

Fact 1: Cockroaches breathe through holes in their sides called spiracles.

Fact 2: Cockroaches cannot see in red light, but they can see in green light very well.

Fact 3: Cockroaches get their sense of smell from their antennae.

Fact 4: A cockroach mouth can smell as well as taste – and it moves from side to side, not up and down the way human mouths do.

Fact 5: Cockroaches can live up to two years.

Fact 6: Some humans are allergic to cockroaches.

Fact 7: The brain of a cockroach is scattered along the underside of its belly. That's why if a cockroach's head is cut off, it can survive for up to a week, and then only dying of thirst.

Fact 8: Cockroaches have been present on Earth for more than 400 million years.

Fact 9: There are approximately 4000 types of cockroach.

Fact 10: Most cockroaches have 18 knees.

Fact 11: Some kinds of cockroaches can hold their breath for 40 minutes.

Fact 12: Cockroaches thrive in nearly every corner of the globe, despite our best efforts to get rid of them.

Fact 13: Cockroaches' eyes are made up of 4000 lenses which allows them to see in all directions at the same time.

GLOSSARY

Abdomen – the largest part of an insect's three-part body; the abdomen contains most of the important organs.

Antennae – a pair of special sense organs found at the front of the head on most insects.

Arthropod – any minibeast that has jointed legs; insects and spiders are arthropods.

Bristles – short, strong hairs.

Decomposers – microscopic plants and animals that break down the dead bodies of other plants and animals.

Exoskeleton – a hard outer covering that protects and supports the bodies of some minibeasts.

Functional – in working order.

Insect – a kind of minibeast that has six legs, most insects also have wings.

Instar – a stage between moults for a developing insect nymph.

Larva – a wormlike creature that is the juvenile (young) stage in the life cycle of many insects.

Microbes – tiny living things, so small that they can only been seen through a powerful microscope.

Minibeast – one of a large number of small land animals that do not have a skeleton.

Moulting – the process of shedding the body's surface layer so that it can be replaced by a fresh one.

Nymph – the juvenile (young) stage in the life cycle of insects that do not produce larvae.

Omnivore – an animal that eats both plants and meat.

Ootheca – egg case produced by female cockroaches.

Parasite – any living thing that lives or feeds on or in the body of another living thing.

Parthenogenesis – the production of young by females without the involvement of males. Some insect species consist entirely of females.

Pheromone – a scent substance produced by many kinds of animals that is used to communicate certain information or "messages".

Predator – an animal that hunts and eats other animals.

Pronotum – a tough shield that protects the head of some cockroaches.

Pupation – the process by which insect larvae change their body shape to the adult form.

Receptors – tiny organs that detect things such as smell, heat, and vibration.

Rotting – the process of decomposition by which the bodies of dead animals and plants are broken down.

Scavenger – an animal that eats dead and rotting plants and animals.

Segment – a part of something that is divided into a number of similar parts.

Skeleton – an internal structure of bones that supports the bodies of large animals such as mammals, reptiles, and fish.

Springtail – a six-legged minibeast which is not a true insect.

Sprinting – running on two legs at top speed.

Subtropical – belonging to a region near Earth's equator where the climate is always warm.

Thorax – the middle part of an insect's body where the legs are attached.

Tropical – belonging to the region around the Earth's equator where the climate is always hot.

index